First Steps to
YOGA

Louise Wiggins

AXIOM

Photographs Michael Lim

With grateful acknowledgement to Geoff Wiggins

ISBN: 1 86476 023 0

Axiom
Australia

Caution: If you have any doubts or concerns about your body's
ability to exercise, please consult your health professional

Disciplined *by yoga practices,*

the mind becomes calm and tranquil. Then the individual self, beholds the true Self and is completely satisfied.

(Bhagavad Gita 6/20)

Contents
page

Listen
to your
Body

Listen to your body,
And wisdom
You will find.
Smile,
And move it
With your breath.
Have a quiet mind.

Follow these instructions
And you'll quickly find,
Yoga's a magic potion
For body,
Breath
And mind.

What Is Yoga

Yoga is a holistic approach to your well being. It is an individual, living experience, with its origins in the East. The various practices of yoga help us to find peace, so we may experience our true Self; ageless, timeless and with infinite potential.

Yoga is the art of taking control of your own physical and mental well being. It is a relaxed system of body movements, done slowly with a free flowing breath and a quiet mind. In practicing Hatha yoga, we experience the body, mind and breath in the Asanas, which are postures that are scientifically designed to work each muscle, joint and ligament in the body, so that stimulated blood circulation nourishes every cell for optimum health and vitality, leaving you feeling physically and psychologically strong and mentally and spiritually at peace.

The word yoga means unite or harness together. In fact, our own word 'yoke' comes from the word 'yoga'. All yoga practices are aimed at creating this sensation of union between all the different aspects of ourselves, so we may experience the body as a whole. During yoga practices you experience this union by allowing the mind, body and breath to flow together in harmony with each other. In this way there is the opportunity to surpass the ego and experience Atman, which is pure consciousness.

Through relaxation, slow yoga exercises, meditation, breathing and visualisation practices, we begin to experience our true selves; a state of exquisite 'beingness' in harmony with the natural world.

Hatha yoga invites you on an inner journey of self-discovery where you'll get to know yourself and listen to the messages your body is trying to send to you. This heightened awareness is the key to good health.

The Eight-Fold Path of Yoga

Between 300-500BC Patanjali formally set out the eight fold path of **Astanga** (eight limbs) yoga. This eight fold path to liberation is also known as **Raja** yoga. Here is a brief outline of the eight limbs:

1. *Yamas*
Abstinences, moral qualities of restraint and control of thought, word and deed, for the harmonious functioning of our society.

2. *Niyamas*
Observances of self-discipline, attitudes and activities. These are rules for personal conduct.

3. *Asanas*
Postures for a healthy functioning body so we may experience stillness during meditation.

4. *Pranayama*
Breath control, breathing practices to help control the movement of Prana, life force.

5. *Pratyahara*
Sense withdrawal, turning inward, to calm and centre. Withdrawing the sense of touch, sound, taste, vision and smell.

6. *Dharana*
Concentration, to control and quieten the activities of the mind. Being one-pointed and focussed.

7. *Dhyana*
Meditation, absorption, the mind no longer wanders. It is controlled and resting in stillness.

8. *Samadhi*
Enlightenment, self realisation, the climax of meditation. The experience of union, oneness, harmony and a connection to all life.

Yoga
teaches that man is like a chariot drawn by horses. The chariot is the body. The horses are the senses. The mind is the driver, driving the chariot in sometimes an undesirable direction. The true Self, however is the passenger, sitting quietly beside the driver. The practices of yoga help us to gain mastery of this team.

Yoga Teaches That...

Breath is life. Life is breath.

Full breath, full life. No breath, no life.

Where the mind touches the body, the cells respond.

Health is a state of harmony and balance of body, mind and spirit.

Health is a free flow of energy through the body and the mind. Happiness is a free flow of energy through life.

Love is a free flow of energy from the heart.

The teacher instructs, the body teaches.

Yoga is the stilling of the activities of the mind.

Old age begins with the stiffening of the spine.

You are as young as your spine is flexible.

The mind is the lord of the senses; the breath is the lord of the mind.

Bliss is the effortless suspension of the breath.

In silence we grow. In stillness we heal.

Thoughts produce actions; actions consequences; consequences desires; desires thoughts, and so on. This is Karma; taking full responsibility for our actions.

The fastest way to stretch, is slowly.

The highest yoga is the work we do each day.

A silent invisible intelligence flows through the body and the mind.

Where the mind goes, energy flows.

Healing lies within the stillness of total relaxation.

Union can be experienced if we allow the mind, body and breath to flow together in perfect harmony.

We are human 'beings' as well as human 'doings'.

A Hindu Legend

There is an old Hindu legend which tells us that long ago, all human beings were once gods. However, when they abused their powers, Brahma, the great Lord of all the gods, decided to take back their divinity and hide it where it would never be found. The problem was, where to find such a hiding place. A council of gods was formed to help solve the problem. In time, they came up with the following suggestion, "Let us bury the divinity of human beings, deep in the ground". But Brahma replied, "No that won't do, because sooner or later it will be dug up and found." Another god proposed, "Let us throw it into the depths of the deepest ocean." But Brahma replied, "No that won't do, because sooner or later they will explore the depths of all the oceans and one day they will find it and bring it to the surface." The council of gods came to the conclusion that there was no place they could safely hide the divinity of human beings, without it one day being found. Eventually, Brahma shook his head and said "I know a place where they will never think to look. We shall hide the divinity of human beings, in the deepest depths of themselves, for it is the only place where they will never look." Since that time, human beings have searched and explored the length and breadth of the universe, seeking in vain for something that can only be found within themselves.

Before You Begin
A Guide to Practicing Yoga
- Do not exercise immediately after eating.
- Wear loose, comfortable clothing.
- Practice in bare feet on a non-slip surface.

Before You Begin

Look forward to some precious time for yourself.

Let each movement flow with your breath.

Keep the breath flowing freely, deeply and rhythmically, feeling it as a free flow of energy.

Never strain, or push yourself too far, but don't limit yourself.

Pain is a signal from your body that you have gone too far.

Modify the practice to suit your unique body.

Don't forget that the body whispers and talks to us before it screams! Tune into the whispers.

Enjoy your yoga practice, so that you'll want to practice regularly.

Your body and mind love being stretched.

Let your free flowing breath connect movement, mind and body with a sensation of relaxation.

Arms too short? Legs too long? Use a belt or strap.

Listen to the sensations of the body. Honour its limitations. Let your natural wisdom guide you.

Be comfortable. Modify the poses to suit your unique body at this time.

Smile, softening the eyes, face and throat.

Work slowly with full attention on the areas targeted.

Experience the flow of energy.

With blood pressure problems, take care not to lower the head below the heart.

Pain and discomfort are warning signals to stop.

If you have any doubts about your body's ability to exercise, please consult your health professional.

It is when you have no time to stretch, that you probably need it most.

Affirmations

Throughout this book, you will find an affirmation for each section. When you practice the poses in a particular section, you may like to repeat the accompanying affirmation, to help focus the mind in a positive direction of your choice.

Negative self-criticism and negative thought patterns raise stress levels, lowers self-esteem and weakens the immune system. Affirmations help to correct this imbalance. Below are some extra examples from which to choose:

I have as much potential for improvement as anyone else.

I love and accept myself as I am.

My life is unfolding just as it should.

My pain is the breaking of the shell that encloses my understanding.

As I breathe in, I breathe in healing energy. As I breathe out, I rid my body of negativity and allow my awareness to dissolve into the stillness of my inner calm.

In calmness I grow. In stillness I heal.

I am centred in equanimity.

I have great inner reserves of strength and power.

In stillness I renew my energy.

Today I open the doors to my calmness and let the footsteps of silence gently enter the temple of all my activities. I perform my duties serenely, saturated with peace.

Let's Begin

In the sections that follow, you'll find a variety of yoga stretches and practices. Please take the time to carefully read the instructions.

Where it is applicable, begin with the **HOW** section as it gives you clear guidelines to follow. If you find your body saying "We're not quite ready for this one yet!" then do the **DOING LESS** example instead. If when doing the **HOW** your breathing is deep and rhythmic and your body asks for a greater challenge, then try the **DOING MORE** example. Always listen to your body. It really is your best teacher. It knows you better than anyone.

You can safely proceed to practice the postures in the order in which they are presented in this book. If however you want to prepare a daily practice routine, please look at pages 50 - 53 for three examples.

Don't forget that your body has taken many years to become what it is today. So be patient with yourself as you reach for your potential.

Here is an old Indian saying that helps remind us we are more than just a body:

If you want to know what your thoughts were like yesterday, look at your body today. If you want to know what your body will be like tomorrow, look at your thoughts today.

Henry Ford once said, *"Whether you think you can, or think you can't, you're right!"*

Now that you're ready, let's take the 'First Steps to Yoga'. Enjoy your journey.

Relaxation Pose *Savasana*

Putting the mind back in the body. Relieving stress and releasing tension. To use at the beginning and end of your practice.

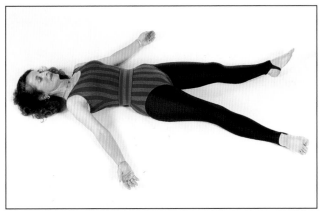

The Relaxation Pose - *Savasana*

Lying on the floor with the spine straight, neck long and the eyes gently closed. The legs are a comfortable distance apart with the feet falling out to the sides, relaxing the hips, knees, ankles and feet. Roll the arms away from the sides of the body with the palms turned upwards and the fingers and thumbs naturally curled, relaxing the shoulders, elbows, wrists and fingers.

Relax the face. The jaw is loose at the hinge, with the lips lightly touching, the teeth a little apart and the tongue resting in the floor of the mouth with the tip against the lower front teeth. The whole face relaxing into a gentle smile. Allow the navel to sink down. Allow the shoulder girdle to broaden, soften and melt into the floor.

Allow the mind to follow the body into relaxation, noticing your relaxed breath as you allow waves of relaxation to flow through your body and mind.

Mind, body and breath, flowing together with all the naturalness which was intended.

14

Limber Up

Full body stretch.
Stretch the arms beyond the
head in two straight lines and
rotate the ankles in both
directions.

Nose to knees on exhalation.
Full spine stretch. Shoulders
down, elbows wide, smile!
Repeat 3 times.

Stretch the hamstring.
Use a strap over the foot and
breathe gently into your best
stretch sensation. The
hamstrings cross the knee joint
and the hip joint, so straighten
the leg, lifting the kneecaps as
you strengthen the thighs. Hold
for 5 slow breaths on each side.

Supine twist.
Let the knees roll one way, the
head the other way, shoulders
down, breathing length and
space into the whole spine.
Hold for 3 slow breaths on
each side.

Abdominals.
Lower back on the floor.
Relax the shoulders with a
space beneath the chin.
Repeat 5 times on exhalation.

Roll from side to side.
Experience the muscles along
both sides of the spine being
massaged from the shoulders
to the waist to the buttocks.

The Seven - Way Stretch

To stretch the spine through its full range of motion.

Up

Interlace the fingers. Breathe in,
turning the palms towards the
ceiling. Chin in, shoulders down,
tailbone lengthening towards the
floor. Lengthen the spine a little
more with each inhalation. Relax
the shoulders and lengthen the
tailbone a little more with each
exhalation. Experience the
lengthening of the whole spine.

One Side

Inhale, reach for the ceiling.
Exhale, shoulders down, neck
long, navel drawn in, pushing the
rib cage over to one side.
Experience the stretch from the
heel to the fingers, opening the
whole side of the body.

Other Side

Inhale, reach for the ceiling.
Exhale, shoulders down, neck
long, navel drawn in, pushing the
rib cage over to the other side.
Experience the stretch from the
heel to the fingers, opening the
whole side of the body.

Backward

Place the hands on the buttocks,
lengthening the low back by
pushing the buttocks down and
the hips forward. Allow the chest
to open with the inhalation and

allow the spine to extend a little further backwards with the exhalation. Experience the front of the spine stretching and lengthening. Keep the knees soft.

Forward

Rest the hands on the thighs, knees bent. Take a moment to elongate the spine with your breath. Now place the abdomen on the thighs and allow the body to cascade forward. Hold the ankles and slowly straighten the legs a little, with the abdomen still resting on the thighs supporting the lumbar back. Allow the legs to straighten a little, if comfortable, keeping the abdomen on the thighs. (See also Page 27)

Twist

With the arms at shoulder height, place the left hand on the right shoulder and gently allow the spine to twist. Follow the movement with your eyes. Repeat on the other side.

Rotate Shoulders

Come back to centre and draw some slow circles with the shoulders. Reverse the direction. Shrug the shoulders up around the ears. Release, relax, let the tension go as you lower the shoulders away from the ears.

Balance and Harmony

Balancing to develop control over the body and to focus the mind, while learning to find the delicate balance between effort and surrender, being and doing, holding on and letting go.

Flying Balance Pose - *Tuladandasana*

Affirmation

My mind, my body, my breath, my feelings are flowing together in perfect balance and harmony.

Mountain Pose *Tadasana*

A pose to practice if you want to improve posture and correct any imbalance in the body. It is this posture that all the other yoga postures aim to improve with regular practice. Slowly, the body will come into alignment as imbalances are corrected. Although it looks easy, it is probably one of yoga's most difficult postures to perfect.

How

With the weight evenly distributed on both feet, allow each inhalation to lift the crown of the head towards the ceiling. Feel grounded and steady, yet growing upwards at the same time. Lift the kneecaps to unlock the knees, and allow the tailbone to lengthen towards the floor with the navel slightly drawn in. Experience a sensation of comfort, strength and support in the whole pelvic girdle. Allow the shoulder girdle to broaden with the shoulder blades sliding down the upper back. Allow the back of the neck to lengthen by drawing the chin in towards the sternum. Ears, shoulders, hips, knees and ankles in line. Soften the eyes, face and throat. Smile.

Tree Pose *Vrksasana*

How

Begin in Mountain Pose. Experience the balance on both feet. Transfer the balance to the right foot, lifting the left foot to the inner thigh of the right leg. Bring the palms of the hands together, stretching the wrists until the elbows and wrists are in line. Focus your gaze about a body length in front. Let the breath flow and keep a quiet mind. Repeat on the other side.

Doing Less

Use a chair or wall for support. Place the foot on the top of the other foot, shin or knee.

Doing More

Place the foot in the groin, in the half lotus position. Extend the arms beyond the head, palms together, reaching upwards, growing.

Taking Care

Balances are challenging. Accept your limitations and enjoy where you are at this time. Use a chair or wall for support if balancing is difficult.

Breathe *Pranayama*

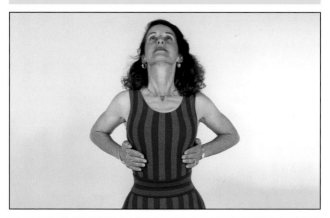

Breathing for SELF
Soft and slow
Easy and even
Long and lingering
Full and free

Prana is the Sanskrit word for life force, or vital energy. It is what keeps us alive. Prana holds our body together. When we stop breathing, the body begins to decompose.
Experience your full breath by allowing your inhalation to fill the lungs from the bottom up. Allow the exhalation to empty the lungs from the bottom up. Experience a full expansion of the rib cage, front back and sides, yet with the shoulders relaxed. Experience new reserves of energy, vitality and enthusiasm. Always breathe smoothly and consciously through the nostrils to experience a free flow of energy through the body and the mind.

Affirmation

My breath is the bridge between my body and my mind.

Moving Breath Meditation

Open the Heart

Enjoy moving your body with your breath. Keep the knees soft and the mind quiet. Enrich your experience of the movements with your breath and your complete attention.

EXHALE

Namaste (see Page 54)
Place the palms of the hands together at the centre of the chest; a place of stillness at the heart centre. Soften the knees. Elbows in line, eyes, jaw, throat relaxed, wrists softening, feeling centred and relaxed.

INHALE

Open the heart
Allow your inhalation to gently open the hands like a book, opening the heart, feeling quiet and focussed, relaxed, centred.

EXHALE

Send Love

Bring the palms of the hands together, closing the hands and slowly extending the arms at shoulder height, sending love. Knees, throat, eyes soft.

INHALE

Receive Love

Open the arms wide, turning the palms up, looking up, receiving love. Experience the joy of receiving as well as giving.

EXHALE

Coming back to Centre

Allow the palms to come together above the head and bring the hands back to the heart centre, bringing the love back to the heart, feeling satisfied, and at peace.

Repeat the Moving Breath Meditation 5 times or more.

Strength and Flexibility

The flexibility we gain from our yoga practice is much more than just physical. Experience this flexibility as it combines with strength to benefit the whole body. *Triangle Pose* has special benefits for the spine, shoulders, legs, chest and the whole nervous system. Allow each breath to give you new strength and energy, and to create space in the body, feeling more and more flexible and strong in body and mind.

Affirmation

I am enthusiastic about life. I am filled with energy and optimism.

Triangle Pose *Utthita Trikonasana*

How

Step the feet apart to make a large triangle with the legs. Turn the left foot out and the right foot in. Extend the arms to shoulder height and glide to the left. Place the left hand along the left leg, lifting the kneecaps, right hand reaching up. Lengthen the back of the neck. Turn the head to see only your thumb. With each inhalation, fill the joints of the body with space. With each exhalation, allow your hand to move a little further down along the left leg while it feels comfortable. Repeat on the other side.

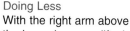

Doing Less

With the right arm above the knee, kneecap lifted, left arm reaching up.

Doing More

With the fingers of the left hand on the floor behind the left leg.

Taking Care

This is a vigorous lateral extension of the spine, so take care not to roll the shoulder forward. Let the chest open, breathing freely and easily. Keep the back leg firmly grounded. With back problems you may be more comfortable bending the front knee. Do a forward bend (next page) as a counter stretch.

Forward Bends

Developing patience, humility and perseverance as the whole back of the body stretches and surrenders into the stillness within. Always bend from the hips, with the knees soft, keeping the spine long and flat. Bending from the waist puts too much load on the lumbar back risking low back injury.

The Back Stretch - *Paschimottanasana*

Affirmation

I surrender. I have trust in the silent invisible intelligence that flows through my body and my mind.

The Cascading Waterfall *Uttanasana*

How

Begin in *Mountain Pose* (Page 19) breathing length and alignment into the spine. Experience the spine's natural curves. Bend the knees, with feet hip width apart, rest a hand on each knee and begin to bend forward keeping the spine straight. Rest the tummy on the thighs to support the lower back. Breath by breath, allow the hands to move towards the ankles and straighten the legs a little at a time. Inhaling, lengthening the spine, tailbone to crown; exhaling a little further forward if it feels comfortable. Enjoy the wonderful stretch sensation along the entire back of the body from the heels to the crown of the head.

Doing Less

Keep the knees soft or bent, focus on elongating the spine, giving it a good traction.

Doing More

Breathing in spaciousness, along the spine breathing out, letting go.

Taking Care

If you have blood pressure problems, don't lower the head below the heart. If your hamstrings are tight, be satisfied to bend forward only a little. Accept your unique body's limitations and don't strain. Don't forget to breathe! Enjoy where you are.

Chin to Knee, Nose to Shin *Janu Sirsasana*

Sitting on the floor, legs extended, lifting yourself up on the sitting bones. Bend the right leg placing the foot against the inner thigh. Place a strap around the sole of the foot, or simply rest the hands on the leg and begin to gently allow the body to extend forward from the hips, keeping the spine flat and long. Draw the navel in for extra support. Surrender as you breathe into your best stretch sensation. Repeat with the other leg.

Doing Less
Relax the shoulders, lift the spine up out of the sitting bones. Breathe length into the spine.

Doing More
With the abdomen resting on the thigh, surrender the chin to the knee and the nose to the shin.

Taking Care

Maintain the natural curves in the spine. If your hamstrings are tight, the spine will round and you'll have frown lines on your waist! Sit on a cushion or on rolled blankets to help tilt the pelvis forward. Let your body's natural intelligence guide you. Be patient. Relax and enjoy the stretch sensation.

Back Bends

Bending over backwards for better breathing, a healthier spine and improved posture. Back bends enliven the spine, opening the chest and heart while stretching the whole front of the body. With the front of the body open, and the shoulders wide, the breath deepens, slows and lengthens. No wonder backbends leave us feeling so exhilarated!

The Camel Pose - *Ustrasana*

Affirmation

I am open and receptive to the infinite possibilities of my life.

Cobra *Bujangasana*

Begin by lying on the front of the body, with the hands under the shoulders, fingers spread wide with the middle fingers pointing straight ahead and the elbows tucked in to the sides. Lengthen the back of the neck, resting the forehead on the floor. Experience your relaxed spine. Gently squeeze the buttocks just enough to lengthen and strengthen the lumbar back, anchor the fronts of the feet and pubis to the floor and slowly begin to lift, shoulders down, elbows in, face soft and smiling.

Doing Less
Sphinx pose, with the forearms resting on the floor, elbows in line with the hands and shoulders.

Doing More
Snake pose, shoulders strengthening as you lift your body's weight off the floor.

Taking Care

Before beginning a backbend, always lengthen the low back by squeezing the buttocks and tucking the tail under while drawing the navel in, without creating tension. Allow the neck to be long, the shoulder girdle to feel spacious as the shoulder blades move down the back ribs. Keep the breath flowing. Smile. Counter stretch by resting in child pose (Page 45). Listen to your body. Don't push yourself too far. Not suitable for pregnancy.

Bridge Pose *Setu Bandhasana*

How

Begin by lying on the floor in the semi-supine position, with the knees bent and in line with the feet and the hips. Walk the heels towards the buttocks, lengthen the back of the neck with the arms resting beside your body. With every inhalation begin to lift a little higher, with every exhalation firm the buttocks and lengthen the lower back. Lift the heart to the ceiling, rolling the shoulder blades towards each other. Interlace the fingers if you have enough room beneath the buttocks.

Doing Less

Low Bridge. See a straight line between the shoulders and the hips. Open the heart, lengthen the spine.

Doing More

Open Bridge. Extend one leg towards the ceiling, lifting as high as your body permits. Smile as you touch the ceiling! Repeat with the other leg,

Taking Care

Pressing the big toes into the floor will prevent the knees from falling out to the sides. Finish your backbends with child pose (Page 45) or hugging the knees to the chest.

Twists

Twisting the spine for better posture, greater vitality and a free flow of energy from the brain to every nook and cranny of the body via an incredible network of nerves. Stretching and twisting the spine, the body's central axis, to relieve tension and release energy. That's why it feels so good to twist the spine all the way from the base of the spine to the neck.

Spinal Twist Pose - Ardha Matsyendrasana

Affirmation

Today I shall judge nothing that occurs. Non-judgement creates stillness in my body and my mind.

Supine Twist

Semi-Supine Position

Allow the spine to soften, with the waist flat on the floor, knees and feet in line with the hips. Neck long, shoulders relaxed. Breathe and relax.

Twist

Bring the feet together and stretch the arms to shoulder height. Let the navel sink down on the exhalation and allow the knees to move to the left as the head rolls to the right, keeping the right shoulder down. Experience your best twist. Enjoy releasing tension. Repeat on the other side.

Straighten the Spine.

Hug the knees to the chest and allow the spine to stretch and straighten. Bring the nose towards the knees, shoulders down, elbows wide, face soft, neck long. It feels so good to stretch and relax.

Sitting Twist *Ardha Matsyendrasana*

How
Sitting on the sitting bones,
so that there are no frown
lines across the belly. Step
the right foot over the left
leg. Place the left hand on
the right knee. If you're
comfortable, elongate the
spine and rest the elbow on
the outside of the knee,
fingers extended. Lengthen
the back of the neck and
twist from the base of the
spine to the neck, drawing

the navel in away from the thigh. Repeat on the other side.

Doing Less
Sit on a bolster, a cushion, a
rolled blanket or on a chair.

Doing More
Bend the left leg and take the
left hand to the lower knee.

Taking Care

Always check that the spine is straight before you allow it to
twist. Experience the spine's natural curves in the lower
back and neck. If you feel that your back is still rounded, sit
on a folded blanket or towel. Use the in breath to elongate
the spine. Use the out breath to twist a little further.

Strength and Determination

Bearing weight on the arms and legs, helps to strengthen the muscles, bones and joints of the whole body while improving posture and circulation.

Arm Balance - *Vasisthasana*

Affirmation

My inner strength gives me great power. I allow it to operate within me knowing that my inner strength is greater than any of my problems.

Warrior *Virabhadrasana II*

Preparation

With the feet wide apart, turn the right foot out and the left foot in. Extend the arms to shoulder height, fingers alive with energy. Use the breath to lift energy from the feet up the legs, along the torso, across the shoulders and into the arms to the fingertips. Allow the strength in the legs to lift the spine up out of the pelvis as your feet ground you to the floor.

Warrior Pose

Keeping the torso perpendicular to the floor, sink down into the strength of warrior pose. Experience the strength from the legs, lifting up the spine, into the arms and through the whole body. Keep the knee over the ankle and in line with the hips, the face soft and the breath freely flowing.

Dog Pose *Adho Mukha Svanasana*

How

Begin with the knees under the hips and the hands under the shoulders, with the middle fingers pointing straight ahead. Step the hands one hand length further forward. Come up on the toes, straightening the legs and look up. Now allow the heels to lower towards the floor as the ears move between the arms. Use the strength in the arms and legs to stretch the spine dynamically. Breathe an energy flow up the arms to the sitting bones and down to the heels. Allow the shoulders to broaden and the shoulder blades to move down the rib cage.

Doing Less

Use your desk, bench, window sill or chair to release shoulder tension and straighten the spine.

Doing More

Lift one leg to the ceiling as the hands press into the floor, ears away from the shoulders. Repeat with other leg.

Taking Care

Draw the navel in, to support the lower back. Lower the shoulders away from the ears. Let the breath flow freely to experience the benefits of this gentle version of the yoga headstand.

Sitting and Centring

For meditation, hip flexibility, centring, aligning the spine and coming into a soft inner focus. It is so easy to find time to practice sitting poses at any time during a busy day. Sitting up, not down, benefits not only the spinal column, but also creates new space for the inner organs as it allows the breath to deepen and slow.

Lotus Pose - Padmasana

Affirmation

I am calm and centred. I have plenty of time for everything.

Preparing to Sit

Rod Posture

Sit with legs extended. Make fists, push them into the floor and lift yourself up onto the sitting bones. Rest the hands on the floor, spine straight and long, shoulders relaxed. Breathe up the spine, removing any frown lines on the belly.

Preparing The Ankles

Hold the foot, rotate the ankle slowly in both directions. Check that the ankles are relaxed by holding the lower leg and shaking the foot loose. Repeat with the other leg.

Preparing The Hips, Knees And External Hip Rotators

Lying down with the knees bent, place the right foot on the left thigh. Lift the left foot from the floor. Thread the right arm between the thighs and clasp the fingers behind the left thigh, or around the left shin. Experience the stretch in the right hip and buttock. Repeat on the other side. The neck is long and the shoulders relaxed.

Easy Posture
Sukhasana

Sit upright with the spine aligned, and on a cushion if there are frown lines on the belly. Cross the ankles and place the left foot under the right knee and the right foot under the left knee. Knees resting on the feet. Hands resting on the knees.

Pose of the Adept
Siddhasana

Place the right heel at the perineum. Place the left heel in front of the right foot, with the heels in line. Allow the knees to sink down toward the floor, as the spine lengthens and straighten a little more with each breath. Rest the hands on the knees.

Cobbler's Pose
Baddha Konasana

Place the soles of the feet together and place the hands on the ankles or around the feet, whichever is more comfortable for you. Breathing in, lengthening the spine. Breathing out, lowering the knees towards the floor. Allow gravity to help you. There is no need to strain.

Inverted Postures

Inversions keep the body in perfect health by invigorating, renewing and rejuvenating the whole being. All inverted postures improve digestion and ease the venous blood flow back to the heart. Inversions regulate blood pressure and improve metabolism through more efficient thyroid function. Dog Pose (Page 37) is also a gentle version of the yoga headstand. All inverted postures are your rejuvenating, revitalising anti-wrinkle poses! So invert your body every day.

Pose of Tranquility

Affirmation

I focus on being thankful. I have much to be thankful for.

Shoulderstand *Ardha Sarvangasana*

How
Lying down on the floor with the knees bent and the backs of the hands under the buttocks, draw the knees to the chest. Straighten the legs and lift the hips, supporting the weight of your body in your hands. As you breathe slowly, deeply and fully, gently allow the elbows to move in line with the shoulders. Take a moment to experience the benefits of being inverted. It is wonderful for tired legs, varicose veins, deep breathing and nourishing all the facial tissues, eyes, throat, ears and brain. The shoulderstand is considered the 'queen' of the yoga position.

Doing Less
Rest the legs up the wall and use this gentle version of the shoulderstand as a relaxing pick-me-up.

Doing More
Draw the chest to the chin and experience a stronger neck stretch and chin lock.

Taking Care

Lower the shoulders away from the ears, lengthening the neck. Let the breath flow freely to experience the benefits. Not suitable for children, pregnancy, blood pressure problems, detached retina, neck or ear problems, or displaced discs.

The Headstand *Sirsasana*

How

Most of my students love this version of the headstand. We call it the 'headless headstand'. Experience the benefits of the headstand without any pressure on the cervical

vertebrae. In fact, the weight of the head actually stretches the neck. Position two padded chairs slightly apart and near a wall. Place the head between the chairs with the shoulders on the middle of the seats. Hold the front edges of the chairs. Step the knees onto the seats. Gently transfer the body weight slightly up and back until the legs feel light.

Draw the navel in, push the hands into the chair and stretch the legs up. Make sure that you have someone standing by when you first try this pose. The headstand is considered the 'king' of the yoga postures. Come out of the posture slowly, bringing the head up last.

Doing Less

The head is lifted just off the floor. Feel the strength in the shoulder girdle.

Doing More

Little bird pose with the knees on the backs of the upper arms.

Taking Care

As with the Shoulderstand, Don't do little bird pose if you have neck problems.

Rest and Renew

Take some time each day to nurture yourself with one of
these restorative postures. Begin and end your daily
yoga practice with one of the poses in this section, so
that you can experience harmony and balance between
the body, mind and emotions. We tend to be such
human doings, that we forget to take time to be human
beings. So relax and experience the present moment.

Inverted Relaxation Pose - Viparita Karani

Affirmation

I know that peace comes not from doing, but from
undoing; not from getting but from letting. Letting go.
I rest in the stillness of my inner calm.

4 Relaxation Poses

Child Pose
Pranatasana
Let the spine lengthen over the thighs. Soften the shoulders with the hands alongside the feet, palms up. Forehead on the floor or on your fists if you have blood pressure problems.

Legs up the Wall
Viparita Karani
Sit sideways near a wall or chair, so that both buttocks are on the wall. Swing the legs up and rest the arms alongside the body away from the ribcage, letting go a little more with each relaxed exhalation.

Supine Cobbler
Supta Baddhakonasana
Lie on a bolster or a rolled blanket, with the soles of the feet together, lower back supported, hips relaxing. Lengthen the back of the neck and allow the shoulder girdle to soften, letting go of stored tension. Use a strap as shown to help lengthen the lower back and release the hips.

Relax the Back
With a rolled blanket or bolster under the knees.

Relaxation Pose *Savasana* See Page 14 for details.

Meditation

Yoga is the ability to still the activities of the mind.
(Yoga Sutra of Patanjali 1.2)
Taking a few minutes each day to pause and meditate,
will allow you to tune into your body's own natural
intelligence. You will come to love and accept the
precious, unique, individual that you are right now, while
revealing the incredible inner strength that you have to
realise your best potential.

Affirmation

In stillness I heal

Meditation

Meditation is a practice to help still the activities of the mind, allowing us to find a calm inner focus; a stillness within. Stillness is the blank canvas on which we paint pictures of our lives. Each day we add more and more layers of ever changing pictures until we forget that blissful nothingness from where we began. Through meditation practices we can permeate all the layers of paint, peel away all the different images to reveal our source, our true nature, our true selves. We begin to realise that the stillness of our blank canvas lies behind all the images we have created. All we have to do, is to quieten the body and the mind, and to slip beneath the images into the stillness of our awareness, a place of infinite wisdom and intelligence and there to experience the oneness of yoga.

To practice meditation, find a comfortable sitting position with the spine straight, resting the hands on the knees or the lap. With the eyes closed, allow your awareness to follow the breath in and out of the nostrils, without letting the mind wander. Experience being in the present moment. Listen to your natural inner wisdom. The meditation below, may help to create in calm inner focus, to help still the activities of the mind.

Breathing Meditation
As I breathe in,
I breathe in healing energy.
As I suspend my breath in,
prana heals my body and my mind.
As I breathe out,
I rid my body of disease, tiredness, tension, toxins, discomfort, mental
problems, confusion and the past.
As I suspend my breath out,
I find stillness, and peace within. I become in touch with my higher
energy, my natural wisdom, the higher power within.

Upanishads

The *Upanishads* are early spiritual gospels. They are the Hindu equivalent of the Christian New Testament. These wonderful stories contain much timeless wisdom. Below are a couple of excerpts to whet your appetite.

Father, what is this knowledge by which all is known? Son, let me show you. Please bring me a fruit from that banyan tree. Here it is father. Son, please break it open and tell me what you see. I see nothing father. It is from this essence that we cannot see, that comes this vast banyan tree. This invisible, subtle essence is the whole universe. That is reality. That is life. That is it. That is *Atman*. You are it. (from the *Chandogya Upanishad*)

The two paths lie in front of man. Pondering on them, the wise man chooses the path of joy; The fool takes the path of pleasure. (from the *Katha Upanishad*)

It is not speech which we should want to know;
we should know the speaker.
It is not things which we should want to know;
we should know the seer.
It is not sounds which we should want to know;
we should know the hearer.
It is not mind which we should want to know;
we should know the thinker.
Kaushitaki Upanishad

Never Too Old

When Fred turned 80, he decided to take up yoga and join his wife, Lorna in my Friday morning class.

Lorna has been coming to class for four years and finds that it not only helps her to relieve arthritic pain, but it also releases new reserves of energy and enthusiasm. She told me recently that it is so encouraging to do something for yourself where you actually see improvement with age. Yoga is helping to dismiss the notion that we deteriorate as we grow older.

Fred and Lorna have recently celebrated their 50th wedding anniversary. It is a delight to see them enjoying life so fully. They have found that yoga is a form of exercise they can enjoy together, to keep their joints limber, the breath flowing freely and the energy levels high. They are an inspiration to all of us.

Fred and Lorna enjoying the triangle pose to keep their bodies strong and flexible

A Daily Practice Routine

Experience the benefits of stretching and strengthening each day, so that you can enjoy reaching for your potential. For best results, practice at the same time each day, in a quiet place where you won't be disturbed. Take the time to develop a routine of practicing some yoga every day to keep you balanced and energised. Your body loves being stretched. It will be forever grateful!

Practice on an empty stomach on a non-slip surface. Refer to page 11 for further guidelines.

On the pages that follow, you will find three different practices for you to try. There is a 10 minute stretch and strengthen routine, a 20 minute restorative routine and a 30 minute balanced practice routine.

In time you'll find yourself making up your own routine of postures and practices. The three examples will help you to develop your own routine so that you keep the practice balanced, doing something from each section.

Look around your area and find a yoga class nearby. You'll still want to continue your own daily practice, but joining a class in enriching and enjoyable, as you share the powerful benefits of yoga with like minded individuals.

10 Minute Daily Practice

STRETCH, STRENGTHEN, ENERGISE
This is a dynamic, energising sequence, to use when you need a pep-me-up. Increase the number of breaths in each pose when you feel ready.

- **Mountain Pose p19** 5 deep slow breaths
- **The Seven-Way Stretch p16**   2 rounds
- **Warrior p32**   5 deep slow breaths on each side
- **Triangle p25**   5 deep slow breaths on each side
- **Cascading Waterfall p27**   5 deep slow breaths
- **Dog Pose p37**   5 deep slow breaths
- **Sitting Twist p34**   5 deep slow breaths on each side
- **Forward Stretch p28**   5 deep slow breaths
- **Semi supine position p33**   deep breathing with the hands resting on the solar plexus
- **Relaxation p14, with affirmation p12** repeating it 3 times, 2 minutes

I have great inner reserves of strength and power. I allow it to operate within me.

20 Minute Daily Practice

RESTORE, RENEW, REJUVENATE, CENTRE
Use this routine after a busy day: as an early morning practice or whenever you need time to restore the body and mind back to equilibrium.

- **Supine Cobbler p45** 10 deep slow breaths
- **Legs up the Wall p45** 10 deep slow breaths
- **Mountain Pose p19** 5 deep slow breaths
- **The Seven-Way Stretch p16**   repeat 3 times moving in harmony with the breath
- **Headless Headstand p43** (or any other inversion such as shoulderstand, dog pose or child pose)   20 deep slow breaths
- **Standing Breath Meditation, opening the heart p22** 5 rounds
- **Relaxation p14, with affirmation p12** repeating it 3 times, 2 minutes

I love and accept myself as I am. My world is unfolding just as it should.

30 Minute Daily Practice

A BALANCED PRACTICE
Whenever you can, use the counting of the exhalations as your calm inner focus.

- **Relaxation P14 with affirmation, p12** repeating it 3 times, 2 minutes
- **The Seven-Way Stretch p16** 2 rounds
- **Limber up** p15
- **Standing Breath Meditation, p22** opening the heart 5 rounds
- **Mountain Pose p19** 5 deep slow breaths, breathing space and alignment into the body
- **Tree Pose p20** 5 breaths each side
- **Triangle Pose p25** 5 breaths each side
- **Cascading Waterfall p27** 5 deep slow breaths

- **Dog Pose p37** 5 deep slow breaths
- **Child pose p45** 5 deep slow breaths
- **Cobbler Pose p45** 5 deep slow breaths
- **Shoulderstand p42** 5 deep slow breaths
- **Bridge Pose p31** 5 deep slow breaths
- **Hug knees to the chest p33** lying down 5 deep slow breaths
- **Sitting twist p34** 5 breaths each side
- **Sitting forward stretch p20** 5 slow deep breaths
- **Meditation p47 in easy pose p40**
- **Relaxation Pose p14** 2 minutes, repeating affirmation 3 times

Visualisation:
Send your mind away to your mental retreat, your own personal, private inner sanctum, where you can be alone and at peace. Accept whatever image comes to mind. See yourself there, happy, contented and peaceful. Seeing yourself exactly how you would like to be. Allowing yourself to have all you need, to be everything you wish to be and to succeed in whatever you wish to be doing. Enjoy the image, and holding that positive picture of yourself for a few minutes longer.

I have as much potential for improvement as anyone else.

Namaste
an eastern greeting

With the palms of the hands together, resting at the heart centre.

I honour the place within you
Where the universe resides.
In love, in truth, in peace.
I honour the place within you,
For if you are in that place in you,
And I am in that place in me,
There is only one of us.

Namaste

Further Reading

The Complete Yoga Book
James Hewitt (Rider)

Awakening the Spine
Vanda Scaravelli (Harper Collins)

Yoga the Iyengar Way
Silva, Mira & Shyam Metha (Simon & Schuster)

Light on Yoga
BKS Iyengar (The Aquarian Press)

The Breathing Book
Donna Farhi (Simon & Schuster)

The Book of Yoga
The Sivananda Yoga Centre (Book Club Associates, London)

The Complete Stretching Book
Maxine Tobias, John Patrick Sullivan (Simon & Schuster)

Back Care Basics
Mary Pullig Schatz MD (Rodmell Press)

The Heart of Yoga
Desikachar (Inner Traditions International)

Runner's World Yoga Book
Jean Couch (Anderson World Inc)

Teach Yourself Yoga
Eve Grzybowski (Simon & Schuster)

The Upanishads
(Penguin)

The Bhagavad Gita
(Penguin)

First Steps To Meditation
Lynn Genders (Axiom)

In Stillness I Heal, My Spine
CD and booklet - Louise Wiggins (Banyan Tree)

The Journey of a Thousand Miles Begins with a First Step...

the First Steps
series

- First Steps to Meditation
- First Steps to Massage
- First Steps to Tarot
- First Steps to Chi Kung
- First Steps to Dream Power
- First Steps to Yoga

Further titles following shortly:

- First Steps to Reflexology
- First Steps to Feng Shui
- First Steps to Managing Stress
- First Steps to Astrology
- First Steps to Chinese Herbal Medicine
- First Steps to Acupressure

First Steps to...

•AXIOM PUBLISHING
Unit 2, 1 Union Street, Stepney, South Australia, 5069